Matters of Opinion

OBESITY

By
STUART A. KALLEN

NORWOOD HOUSE PRESS
CHICAGO, ILLINOIS

Norwood House Press
P.O. Box 316598
Chicago, Illinois 60631

For information regarding Norwood House Press, please visit our website at:
www.norwoodhousepress.com or call 866-565-2900.

LIBRARY OF CONGRESS CATALOGING-IN-PUBLICATION DATA

Kallen, Stuart A., 1955- author.
  Obesity / by Stuart Kallen.
    pages cm. -- (Matters of opinion)
  Audience: Ages 8-12.
  Audience: Grades 4 to 6.
  Summary: "Explores pros and cons of several issues related to obesity
including; who's at fault, government prevention, and effective treatments.
Aligns with Common Core Language Arts Anchor Standards for Reading
Informational Text, Speaking and Listening. Text contains critical thinking
components for social issues and history. Includes bibliography, glossary,
index, additional resources and instructions for writing an opinion-based
essay"-- Provided by publisher.
  Includes bibliographical references and index.
  ISBN 978-1-59953-756-6 (library edition : alk. paper) -- ISBN
978-1-60357-864-6 (ebook)
1. Obesity--Juvenile literature. 2. Medical policy--Juvenile literature.
3. Dietetics--Juvenile literature. I. Title. II. Series: Matters of
opinion.
  RC628.K285 2016
  616.3'98--dc23
                                                    2015027483

289N—062016
Manufactured in the United States of America in Brainerd, Minnesota.

Contents

Note: Words that are **bolded** in the text are defined in the glossary.

Timeline

1960 ▸ Around 33 percent of US adults are overweight, and 10 percent are considered obese.

1967 ▸ The first gastric bypass surgery is performed when a patient's stomach is stapled so it will hold less food.

1970 ▸ High fructose corn syrup is introduced to the United States to be used as a substitute for sugar in food items such as soda.

1971 ▸ Around 5 percent of American kids are obese.

1990 ▸ Overweight and obese adults make up 50 percent of the population in the United States.

1996 ▸ The first bariatric bypass surgery is performed.

1998 ▸ The National Institutes of Health adopts new body mass index guidelines, lowering the healthy weight number from 27 to 25. After the change 25 million more Americans are classified as overweight.

1999 The hospital costs for treating diseases in obese kids reaches $127 million.

2000 Annual sugar consumption in America reaches an average of 150 pounds (68kg) per person, around 38 times more sugar than the average American ate in 1900.

2008 According to the World Health Organization, 1.4 billion adults are overweight worldwide, 500 million are obese, and 2.8 million die annually from weight-related issues.

2010 First Lady Michelle Obama starts the Let's Move campaign to end childhood obesity.

2015 About 33 percent of American kids and 63 percent of adults are either overweight or obese.

1 What Are the Issues with Obesity?

Writer Courtney E. Martin calls the modern era the "age of **obesity**."[1] And it seems like the topic is in the news almost every day. Newspapers, news shows, magazines, and the Internet are flooded with obesity studies. They also have a lot of obesity statistics and cures. If someone searched online for the phrase "obesity is caused by," they would get more than 61 million results.

Measuring a Trend

Study after study has shown that people around the world are getting heavier. In 1990 **overweight** and obese adults made up 50 percent of the US population. By 2015 that number had grown to 63 percent. That is about two out of three people. According to a Gallup-

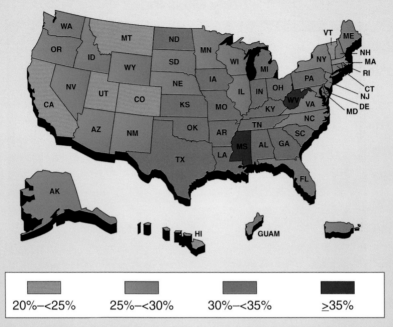

State Obesity Prevalence, 2013

| 20%–<25% | 25%–<30% | 30%–<35% | ≥35% |

Taken from: Centers for Disease Control.

Healthways survey, 35 percent of American adults are considered overweight. And another 28 percent are obese. Around 6 percent of obese people are considered severely obese. They are more than 100 pounds (45kg) overweight, and figures were higher for some groups. The Centers for Disease Control and Prevention (CDC) says the obesity rate among African Americans is nearly 48 percent, and the rate among Hispanics is 42 percent.

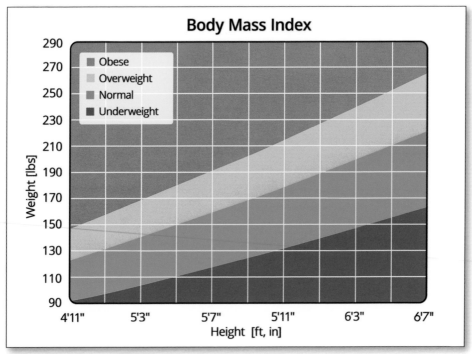

Body Mass Index

Legend:
- Obese
- Overweight
- Normal
- Underweight

Y-axis: Weight [lbs] — 90, 110, 130, 150, 170, 190, 210, 230, 250, 270, 290

X-axis: Height [ft, in] — 4'11", 5'3", 5'7", 5'11", 6'3", 6'7"

The BMI (body mass index) began to be widely used in the early 1970s. Its use today is controversial.

The Body Mass Index

The figures on obesity are based on the accepted definitions of the terms *overweight* and *obese*. These are determined by a guide called the body mass index, or BMI. The BMI measures body fat based on height and weight.

Using a complex formula, the BMI gives a number between 18 and 50. A BMI of less than 18 means a person is underweight. A BMI between 18 and 25 means a person has a healthy weight. And a BMI between 25 and 30 means a person is overweight. A BMI between 30 and 40 is obese, and 41 and over is severely obese.

Did You Know

The Obesity Stigma

Many people who are overweight suffer from an obesity stigma. This includes prejudice and negative attitudes toward those who are obese. The stigma affects kids, teens, and adults. They are made to feel shame, disgrace, or rejection due to their body size. The stigma can involve hurtful words. Some obese people are taunted, teased, made fun of, or called offensive names. The stigma can take physical forms such as unwanted touching and aggressive actions. This includes grabbing, pushing, and punching.

In kids the obesity stigma can lead to social rejection. It can also lead to poor relationships with peers and poor grades. For adults the obesity stigma can cause job discrimination. Obese people are much more likely to report job discrimination due to the stigma. This occurs when obese workers are denied jobs due to body size, in spite of being qualified for the job.

As with many obesity issues, the BMI is controversial. The BMI began to be widely used in the early 1970s. At first American health experts considered a BMI up to 27 healthy. But in 1998 the National Institutes of Health (NIH) adopted new guidelines. The NIH lowered the healthy weight number to 25. Overnight, around 25 million Americans went from being of healthy weight to being overweight.

But the BMI does not tell the whole story. The number does not reveal how much of a person's body weight is healthy muscle and how much is unhealthy fat. That means some lean, muscled athletes and movie stars have high BMIs. For instance, actor Tom Cruise is 5 feet 7 inches tall and weighs 200 pounds (91kg). This gives Cruise a BMI of 31.5. That classifies him as obese. Anyone who has seen Cruise perform his own stunts in action films like *Jack Reacher* knows that the muscular actor is far from obese.

Obesity Health Issues

Most people are not as athletic as Cruise. So the BMI index is reliable for around 90 percent of people. And the NIH says those who are overweight or obese face a lot of health problems. Obese people have a higher risk of coronary heart disease. This can cause heart attacks and heart failure. They are also at a higher risk for strokes and **osteoarthritis** (joint problems). And they are at a higher risk for colon, breast, kidney, and other cancers.

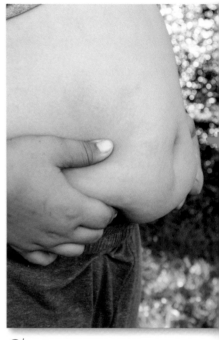

Obesity causes many health problems.

Obesity is also a leading cause of type 2 diabetes. This disease occurs when the level of the body's blood glucose, or blood sugar, is too high. Type 2 diabetes can lead to stroke, kidney disease, limb amputation, and blindness. Around 30 million Americans have type 2 diabetes. That is nearly one in ten people. And there are around 1.5 million new cases every year. But the disease can be prevented. Most diabetes cases are blamed on excess weight, poor diets, and lack of physical activity.

People of some racial and ethnic groups are at a higher risk for type 2 diabetes. The disease is more common among Native Americans, African Americans, Hispanics, and Asian Americans.

Childhood Obesity

Since 1985 obesity rates among kids under 12 have doubled. And the number of obese kids aged 12 to 19 has quadrupled. In 2015 around one in three kids were overweight or obese. And obese kids are much more likely to become obese adults. This has led the *American Journal of Preventive Medicine* to warn that by 2030,

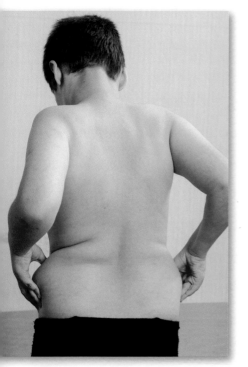

42 percent of Americans will be obese and 11 percent will be severely obese.

As childhood obesity has gone up, so has the number of kids with type 2 diabetes. And this disease is only one of the long-term risks of obesity for

As American adults' obesity rates have increased greatly, so have the obesity rates for children.

kids. Around 70 percent of obese kids have an increased risk of heart disease. They are also at risk for adult health problems such as stroke, several types of cancer, and osteoarthritis.

Matters of Dispute

The food and beverage industry is often blamed for the growing number of obese people. Some diet experts have called for special "fat taxes" on cakes, candy, chips, and soda. They say that making high-fat, low-nutrition food cost more will make people want it less.

Other ideas include putting **regulations** on TV ads aimed at kids. Research shows that TV ads for sweetened cereals, unhealthy snack food, and fast-food chains are making kids fat. Most kids see more than ten food-related ads every day. That is nearly 4,000 a year. And the more food ads kids see, the more likely they are to try those foods and keep eating them. Marion Nestle is chair of the Department of Nutrition, Food Studies, and Public Health at New York University. She says, "Recommendations about healthy eating are overwhelmed by the hundreds of billions of dollars worth of advertising for junk foods that we're subjected to at home and even in public schools."[2]

A Complex Problem

Some people have a contrasting view. They say that regulations will not change people's behavior. Gurpreet Dhaliwal is a professor of clinical medicine. He states, "No government action will directly alter someone's decisions about eating and exercise. Education efforts have not worked, and we can't regulate, legislate or **litigate** any citizen's access to . . . **calories** or choices around exercise."[3]

Those who support this view say government intervention is not needed. Food producers are already taking steps to reduce the unhealthy impact of their foods and drinks. In 2014 the three largest soda makers pledged to cut the number of calories Americans drink by one-fifth by 2025. Coca-Cola, PepsiCo, and the Dr. Pepper Snapple Group said they will offer more low- and no-calorie drinks. They will sell sugary drinks in smaller portions. They will also use ads to educate people and encourage them to drink less soda.

One of Americans' favorite beverages is soda. Unfortunately, the drink is loaded with sugar and calories.

The trade group American Beverage Association (ABA) says obesity is a complex problem. The ABA says it is caused by many factors, "the most important being diet, physical activity and genetics. The key to living a healthy lifestyle is to incorporate a varied, healthy diet that balances calories consumed and calories burned through activity and exercise."[4]

What to Do

The American public is divided when it comes to obesity. A 2013 poll by the Pew Research Center showed that 63 percent believe obesity has consequences, not just for the overweight but for all of society. In spite of this concern, people are divided almost equally on what to do about it. For instance, 54 percent of those

Did You Know

Fruits, Vegetables, and Children's Health

Growing bodies need fruit and veggies to thrive. The US Department of Agriculture (USDA) says kids should eat 1.5 to 2.5 cups of veggies a day, depending on their age and sex. The USDA says fruits and veggies are filling but low in fat and calories. So they help kids reduce the risk of obesity. They also improve kids' nutrition. Because they are rich in vitamins, minerals, and other healthy compounds, these foods have even been shown to boost performance in school. Kids who eat plenty of fruits and veggies do better on tests than those who do not.

polled think that the government should not be involved in reducing obesity. But 42 percent think the government has a role to play.

A Look Inside This Book

The human body comes in a wide variety of shapes and sizes, and the effects of diet and exercise are different for each person. Perhaps this is why the issues surrounding obesity are so complex. A weight-loss solution aimed at one person might not work for the next. Tens of millions of people deal with obesity issues. So it is not surprising that there are so many opinions about causes and solutions. In this book three issues will be covered in more detail: Is obesity the fault of the food industry? Can the government prevent obesity? Is dieting an effective treatment for obesity? Each chapter ends with a section called **Examine the Opinions**, which highlights one argumentation technique used in the chapter. At the end of the book, readers can test their skills at writing their own essay based on the book's topic. Notes, glossary, a bibliography, and an index in the back provide additional resources.

2 Is Obesity the Fault of the Food Industry?

Yes: The Food Industry Makes Billions Selling High-Fat, High-Sugar Foods That Are Addictive

In 2013 the magazine *Scientific American* published an article that linked obesity to addiction. The article was written by Paul J. Kenny. He is an addiction expert. He says that overeating stimulates a part of the brain called the reward center. This area of the brain gives a sense of pleasure and well-being. It does this by secreting a **hormone** called dopamine. This hormone is increased when someone has sex, takes drugs, or drinks alcohol. Kenny says, "Overeating juices up the reward systems in our brain—so much that in some people it overpowers the brain's ability to tell them to stop eating when they have had enough. As with alcoholics and drug addicts, the more they eat, the more they want."[5]

Eating high-calorie, high-fat foods is one reason Americans are overweight.

An Imbalance of Hormones

There are many hormones that work in the body to regulate how much a person eats. Hormones drive a hungry person to search for food. They create a sense of pleasure when a person eats. When enough food has been eaten, a hormone called leptin is released in the gut. This gives a person a feeling of fullness. It also makes food seem less attractive. The person then stops eating and moves on to other things. For thousands of years of human history, the hormone system worked just fine. But Kenny says that "modern, appetizing foods—dense in fat and sugar and often visually appealing—affect reward systems strongly enough to override the appetite-**suppressing** hormones, thus prompting us to eat."[6]

The Flavor "Bliss Point"

Many modern processed foods have been developed to trick the food-processing hormones in the human body. Processed foods are not like basic food items such as apples or steak. They are altered with natural and human-made chemicals. These make the foods look, smell, and taste better. In the 21st century about 70 percent of all foods sold in the grocery store are processed foods. These are developed in high-tech labs.

Food engineers use math models to enhance taste and make foods hard to resist. Howard Moskowitz is a food industry consultant. He says food makers often add salt, fat, or sugar to a product to make what is called a "bliss point."[7] This is a point at which people enjoy a food so much that they can keep eating it without feeling full. Such foods can overwhelm the brain and become addictive.

Corn-Based Sugar Is Addictive

People have eaten sugar made from the sugarcane plant for thousands of years. But in recent years naturally produced cane sugar has been replaced by a sweetener called high fructose corn syrup (HFCS).

In 2013 Canadian experts studied HFCS. They found that it causes reactions in rats like those made by addictive drugs. Experiments show the corn sugar triggers the same pleasure centers in the brain as cocaine, morphine, and heroin. Rebecca Cooper is an eating disorder specialist. She says the rats in the experiment acted much like drug addicts. They had "intense craving, the inability to control or stop use . . . and withdrawal symptoms" when the HFCS was removed from their diets.

Rebecca Cooper, "Sugar and High Fructose Corn Syrup: Not Such a Sweet Deal," *Huffington Post*, November 28, 2012. www.huffingtonpost.com.

"Keep Eating It Forever"

The food industry uses thousands of chemists and technicians to devise the most appealing foods. Steve Witherly is a food scientist and author of *Why Humans Like Junk Food*. He says a popular puffed cheese snack

A single 2-ounce serving (57g), about 21 pieces, of cheese puffs has half the daily fat and salt that kids should eat. Cheese puffs have 320 calories per serving.

has the perfect ingredients to reach the bliss point. After eating the cheese puffs, he said: "This is one of the most marvelously constructed foods on the planet, in terms of pure pleasure. . . . [It melts in your mouth.] If something melts down quickly, your brain thinks that there's no calories in it . . . you can just keep eating it forever."[8]

It is easy to see how people become addicted to cheese puffs and other snacks with little nutritional value. Junk food overwhelms the hormones that stop people from eating when they are full. Experts work to create a bliss point in everything from yogurt to soup and soda. So it is easy to see that the food industry is to blame for obesity.

But Not So Fast....

No: Individuals, Not the Food Industry, Are to Blame for Rising Rates of Obesity

In 2013 a 56-year-old man from New York City filed a lawsuit against four fast-food chains. He said that his addiction to their food led to his obesity. It also led him to have two heart attacks and develop type 2 diabetes. Steven Anderson works with the National Restaurant Association trade group. He says, "Restaurants have a wide variety of choices on their menus, and people make the choice to eat what they want and when they want every day. This is all about personal responsibility and moderation."[9]

Many agree that those who eat lots of unhealthy foods are not taking responsibility for their actions. And

Americans eat out more than ever, and restaurant meals are often full of hidden fats.

those who say they are addicted to food cannot back their claims with scientific evidence. Gabriel Harris is a professor of food science at North Carolina State University. He says that the human brain is "wired" to respond to certain tastes, textures, and colors in food. But, he says, "that doesn't mean it's an addiction. . . . Abusing drugs doesn't affect brain chemistry in the same way. So making a general statement that foods affect the brain in the same way as drugs would be false."[10] In other words, bad diets are a matter of poor eating habits, not addiction.

People Need to Get More Exercise

In 2014 the Stanford University School of Medicine did a study. It showed that fattening food and drinks may not be the cause of the surge in obesity. Rising rates of obesity have matched the rise of sedentary lifestyles over the past few years. The study showed that around 11 percent of men said they did not exercise at all in 1988. In 2010 the number of men who did not exercise jumped nearly four times to 43 percent. Similar numbers were reported by women. During that same period adult obesity rates went from around 20 percent to 35 percent. Yet the number of calories consumed by adults had not changed much since the late 1980s. Uri Ladabaum was the lead author of the study. He says, "Our findings support the notion that exercise and physical activity are important [factors] of the trends in obesity."

Quoted in Becky Bach, "Lack of Exercise, Not Diet, Linked to Rise in Obesity, Stanford Research Shows," Stanford Medicine, July 7, 2014. http://med.stanford.edu.

Inactivity is another reason for high obesity rates.

Healthy Choices, Bad Diets

Food makers offer many healthy products to people who wish to buy them. Fast-food chains have foods such as salads and grilled chicken on their menus. And grocery store aisles are filled with foods made with whole grains, beans, lean meats, fruits, veggies, and low-fat dairy products.

The problem is that millions of people do not include these foods in their diets. Harris says, "There are no bad foods, but there are bad diets. Consuming certain foods is fine as long as they are consumed in moderation and not all the time. To enjoy these things occasionally is reasonable. That's [the] kind of balance we need to aim for."[11]

The Role of Parents

In 2013 the Gillings School of Global Public Health at the University of North Carolina did a study. It showed that obesity does not begin at the grocery store or fast-food restaurant. Obesity begins at home. The report looked at obesity in kids. It found that bad dietary choices are taught to kids at an early age by parents and caregivers.

The Gillings study found that obese kids were mainly fed processed food and sugar-sweetened drinks at home. The kids were rarely offered fruits or veggies. Barry Popkin is a nutritionist. He says the lack of healthy meals at home "is really what is driving children's obesity. Eating fast foods is just one behavior that results from those bad habits. Just because children who eat more fast food are the most likely to become obese does not prove that calories from fast foods bear the brunt of the blame."[12]

Closing Argument

Whether the food industry makes addictive food and causes obesity or whether obesity is the result of people's choices is an issue. Some think that food companies purposely make addictive foods. These foods are high in salt, sugar, and fat. These overwhelm the brain's ability to regulate how much a person eats. Others say that food is not addictive. They say obese people need to eat better food and exercise more. As the number of public health problems that stem from obesity grow, these issues will long remain subject to debate.

Examine the Opinions

Cause and Effect

In the first essay of this chapter, the author uses an argumentation technique called cause and effect. The author states a cause: The food industry manipulates its products to be irresistibly delicious. The author then associates the cause with an effect; certain foods are addictive, so people are obese. But the author introduces a fallacy, or mistaken belief, when he says that one thing causes another just because both things occur at the same time. This does not make the author's argument wrong. But the reader must examine cause and effect arguments in essays to make sure they make sense.

In the second essay, the author tries to disprove this cause and effect argument. He states that obesity has many causes. These include poor dietary choices, lack of nutritional education at home, and sedentary lifestyles. Plus, food cannot be addictive. So obesity is a matter of personal responsibility. It is not the effect of a single cause. Thus, the author offers many causes for obesity.

3 Can the Government Prevent Obesity?

Yes: The Government Should Do More to Prevent Obesity

In 2014 voters in Berkeley, California, passed a measure. It added a tax of one cent per ounce to sugar-sweetened drinks sold in the city. Someone there who buys a single 12-ounce (340g) can of soda for 99 cents will pay $1.11. A 68-ounce (2L) bottle of soda that sells for 99 cents will cost $1.67 with the tax.

Soda Taxes Can Yield Good Results

The Rudd Center for Food Policy and Obesity is a nonprofit research group. One Rudd Center study says there are many good outcomes from a penny-per-ounce

Berkeley voters celebrate the passage of a law that adds a one cent per ounce soda tax.

soda tax. When soda costs more, people drink less of it. In Mexico, 33 percent of the population is obese. There, a new tax of one peso per liter of soda was enacted in January 2014. After the tax went into effect, soda sales fell by about 8 percent.

Even a small drop in soda sales can reduce public health costs. Mandy Hillstrom is a nutrition professor. She says, "If we reduced consumption even a little bit, it would save pounds and it would save lives."[13] This statement is backed by a group of experts at the University of California and the San Francisco General Hospital and Trauma Center. These experts studied the effects of a national soda tax in the United States. They say that over ten years, a soda tax would prevent 2.4 million cases of diabetes, 100,000 cases of heart disease, and 8,000 strokes. It would also prevent 26,000 deaths. The result would be a $17 billion savings in health-care costs.

Cut the TV Ads

The government can do more than tax soda. It can ban ads for fatty foods and fast foods on kids' TV shows. The American Academy of Pediatrics says most eight- to ten-year-olds spend nearly eight hours a day watching TV and other media. Teens spend eleven hours a day. During these hours kids are not active. They see lots of ads for sugary cereals, fast food, fatty snacks, and other high-calorie foods. Victor Strasburger is a doctor. He says, "We created a perfect storm between media use, junk and fast food advertising, and physical inactivity."[14]

Food makers and fast-food chains spend nearly $2 billion a year on these ads because they know that the

Food Ads Aimed at Children Are Very Effective

McDonald's is the number one advertiser on kids' TV. Most kids aged two to eleven see 245 ads a year for the chain. And it is not the only fast-food chain that advertises on kids' shows. Kids also see hundreds of ads a year from Subway, Burger King, Taco Bell, and other fast-food chains. Fast-food chains spend billions on ads that show fatty foods to kids. So obesity will remain a problem. Jennifer Harris is a food researcher. She says, "[Fast-food] advertising promotes unhealthy regular menu items and often takes unfair advantage of young people's vulnerability to marketing, making it even tougher for parents to raise healthy children."

Quoted in Ryan Jaslow, "Despite More Options, 1% of Fast Food Kids' Meals Healthy," CBS News, November 8, 2013. www.cbsnews.com.

ads work. Glenn D. Braunstein is a doctor. He says ads aimed at kids work because of what is called "pester power." This is when kids keep nagging their parents until they buy an advertised product.

In 2013 First Lady Michelle Obama addressed this issue. She called on companies to stop advertising junk

First Lady Michelle Obama visits a school cafeteria. She has called on companies to stop advertising junk food to kids.

food to kids. She also wanted advertisers to stop using kids' TV characters in ads for unhealthy food. Obama says, "The average child watches thousands of food advertisements each year, and 86% of those ads are for products loaded with sugar, fat, and salt. By contrast, our kids see an average of just one ad a week for healthy products like water or fruits and vegetables. Just one ad a week."[15]

There have been many such calls by the First Lady, doctors, nutritionists, and parents. In spite of these calls, the government has done little.

But Not So Fast....

 No: Government Policies Cannot Reduce Obesity

In 2014 Representative Rosa DeLauro of Connecticut proposed a law. It is called the SWEET Act. This act would impose a one-cent tax on every ounce of sugar-sweetened soft drinks sold in the United States. DeLauro says, "When a two-liter cola is 99 cents and blueberries are over three dollars, something has gone very wrong."[16]

There is one problem with DeLauro's statement. A pint of blueberries has 40 grams of natural sugar. That is about the same amount of sugar as a pint of soda has. And no one is talking about taxing fruit. Also, soda taxes do not apply to fruit juices. These often have more calories than soda. For instance, a cup of orange juice has 112 calories. And grape juice packs 152 calories, according to the US Department of Agriculture. The same amount of cola has 100 calories. Susan Jebb is a diet and obesity expert. She

Fruit juices often contain more sugar than regular sodas.

says, "[Fruit juice] has as much sugar as many classical sugar drinks. It is also absorbed very fast, so by the time it gets to your stomach your body doesn't know whether it's Coca-Cola or orange juice."[17] Other high-calorie drinks would also escape the SWEET tax. These include beer, soy- and dairy-based drinks, iced tea, and sports drinks.

A Tax on the Poor

Taxes on any type of food or drink unfairly tax the poor. The reason poor people drink more soda is that soft drinks are cheaper than healthier drinks such as milk. Little wonder that the general public is not in favor of a national soda tax. A 2014 Rasmussen poll says only one in five Americans supported DeLauro's proposed SWEET tax.

Soda Taxes Do Not Work

Jason Fletcher is a health economist. In 2014 he did a study to find out if soda taxes help reduce obesity.

In 2014 Congresswoman Rosa DeLauro proposed a SWEET tax that would impose a tax on sugary soft drinks. Only one in five Americans agreed with her.

Soda Taxes Punish Low-Income Families

In 2010 the state of New York tried to enact a penny-per-ounce tax on soda. The measure was strongly opposed by the New York City Food Bank. The bank provides hunger relief for the poor. Carly Rothman works at the Food Bank. She explains its view on soda taxes:

> The soda tax might make the sugary drinks less appealing, but it would do nothing to lower the cost of healthy alternatives like milk or vitamin-rich juices, nor improve food access in neighborhoods without supermarkets or grocery stores. . . . [The tax] would punish low-income families for buying soda without offering better alternatives. Meanwhile, the tax will cut into families' limited food dollars, making it even harder to afford healthy foods like fruit, vegetables, whole grains, and low-fat dairy products.

Carly Rothman, "New York Soda Tax Would Hurt, Not Help, Low-Income Families," New York Food Bank, March 15, 2010. www.foodbanknyc.org.

He studied data from Ohio and Arkansas. These states enacted soda taxes in the early 1990s. He compared obesity rates in those states with states where there is no soda tax. He found no difference in rates of obesity.

People in Ohio and Arkansas who could not afford soda just switched to other sugar-sweetened items that were not taxed. Fletcher says, "Given that people substitute other calories when they give up soda, these new results suggest we need [to abandon] policies that make large soda taxes a key element in the fight to reduce overall obesity rates."[18]

TV Ad Bans Do Not Work

Other government efforts to reduce obesity seem to not work well, either. Many people call for a government ban on junk food ads during kids' TV programs. But the

The link between obesity and fast food advertising for kids has not altered the obesity rates in children.

link between the two is weak. Obesity rates have stayed about the same for years. But kids are seeing fewer ads due to changes in viewing habits. There is an increased use of digital video recorders today. So kids are using the fast-forward button to skim through ads. The Rudd Center says this means kids ages six through eleven see about 10 percent fewer fast-food ads than they did in 2012.

Closing Argument

Government bodies oversee many parts of modern life. They levy income taxes, post speed limits on roads, and make sure medicines work and are safe. But whether the government can reduce obesity remains an issue. Those who say yes support taxing sodas and limiting food ads to kids. Others say that government regulations will have little or no effect on peoples' eating habits. Meanwhile, many cities are thinking about charging soda taxes. And public interest groups continue to call for ad bans. As the issues heat up, both sides can expect to engage in an extended debate.

Examine the Opinions

Emotional Appeal

Emotions can act as strong factors when issues are debated. The author of both these essays makes emotional appeals to persuade readers to support the points. The first essay invokes the emotions of happiness and **anticipation**. The author implies that thousands of people will remain healthy and live longer if a national soda tax is enacted. The author also appeals to the reader's sense of fear and disgust when he says that the health of innocent kids is harmed because of TV ads for fast food and junk food. The second essay also appeals to emotions. It cites hardships that a soda tax would inflict on the poor. People might feel sad or angry when they think of poor people being forced to pay higher taxes.

Debaters often turn to the emotional appeal. This is because it is an easy way to persuade readers. People who are scared, anxious, surprised, or even joyful may make decisions that are not based on facts. This may be why so many political ads use emotional appeals. Being able to spot and reject an appeal to the emotions is a good way to avoid being tricked during a debate.

4 Is Dieting an Effective Treatment for Obesity?

 Yes: Dieting Is an Effective Treatment for Obesity

It is a simple fact that people lose weight when they eat fewer calories than they burn in a day. Obese people gain weight because they eat more calories than their bodies need. For instance, 25-year-old Melissa Morris once weighed 673 pounds (305kg). She often ate two or three times more calories than she needed. Her husband Chris describes a single meal for her: "It would be nothing for me to bring home 2 Big Macs, 20 McNuggets, chocolate bars, and soda pop."[19]

Dieting is often hard. But obese people like Morris can lose weight by reducing their caloric intake. Morris lost weight when she gave up sugary sodas. She also

Counting calorie intake is an important part of dieting.

ate grilled chicken or fish rather than fatty fast-food hamburgers.

Testing Diets

In 2014 the Arnold School of Public Health set out to test the value of various diets. The school came up with three different diets for a group of 63 obese people. Twenty-one people were assigned reduced-calorie meat-based diets.

These included low-fat meats, dairy products, and eggs. A second group ate a vegan plant-based diet. The third group followed a plant-based diet but also ate seafood, eggs, and dairy products.

Vegans Lose Weight

The results of the Arnold School study surprised researchers. After eight weeks, those on the vegan diet lost the most weight, around 10 pounds (4.5kg). Those who ate meat and dairy products lost around 5 pounds (2.3kg). Unlike the meat eaters on a low-calorie diet, the vegans said that they did not feel hungry all the time. Researchers say this is due to the fact that vegan diets are high in fiber. This is dietary material, also called roughage. It is found in fruits, veggies, and whole grains.

Fiber-rich foods help people feel full after a meal. The lead author of the study was Gabrielle Turner-McGrievy. She says vegan diets allow the obese "to eat when they are hungry and until they are full, without having to track calories."[20]

Losing Weight on a Vegan Diet

Victoria Moran is an author and health counselor. She calls herself an "obesity survivor." She spent the first 30 years of her life bingeing and dieting until she carried more than 220 pounds (100kg) on her five-foot-two-inch frame. Moran found she could not lose weight by dieting until she switched to a vegan diet. This helped her lose 60 pounds (27kg). She says:

> I was . . . astounded by how well I could eat when I built my menus around vegetables, fruits, whole grains, beans, and a few nuts and seeds. I could finally eat enough. . . . I could eat really big salads and regular-sized portions of veggie-burgers and veggie-chili and veggie-tofu-stir-fries over brown rice. The promise of a thousand [weight-loss] infomercials, "Eat all you want and lose weight," had finally been fulfilled.

Victoria Moran, "The Vibrant Vegan Life of an Obesity Survivor," *Huffington Post*, June 19, 2012. www.huffingtonpost.com.

Vegan diets are high in dietary fiber.

A Lifetime Commitment

Several subjects in the Arnold School study permanently changed their lifestyles. Instead of constantly focusing on calories and dieting, they became committed vegans. Warren Huberman is a weight-loss consultant. He says, "When you are obese, weight control must become a lifetime commitment, and it must involve a decision to completely change the role of food in your life."[21]

There is little doubt that making such a commitment can be hard. But thousands have done so. Whether it is a vow to be vegan or a plan to stick to some other healthy regime, dieting can be an effective treatment for obesity.

But Not So Fast.....

No: Dieting Is Not an Effective Treatment for Obesity

Lisa Goetze used to weigh 550 pounds (249kg). This meant she was morbidly obese. When she was a child, her mother constantly monitored her diet. She limited her food intake and criticized her for eating. Goetze says, "If it were an official category in the *Guinness Book of World Records*, I'd hold the title for the most diets attempted in a lifetime."[22]

It was doubtful that a vegan diet, or any other type of diet, could help Goetze. She finally lost weight after

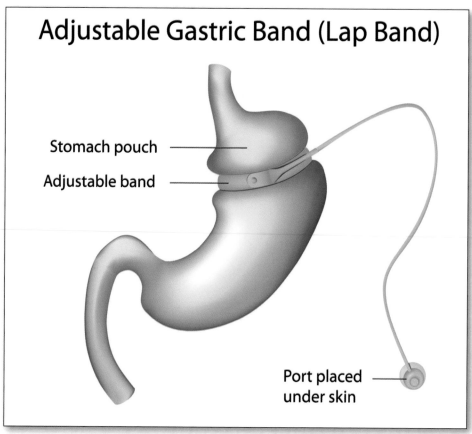

Adjustable Gastric Band (Lap Band)

Stomach pouch

Adjustable band

Port placed under skin

Weight-loss surgery reduces the size of the stomach and limits the amount of food a person can eat.

having weight-loss surgery. This involves dividing the stomach until it is the size of an egg and stapling it. Those who have had this type of surgery can only eat a small amount of food. And they can lose up to 70 percent of their body weight. In the eighteen months after her operation, Goetze lost 350 pounds (159kg).

Nutritional Deficiencies

Supporters of diets often cite the Arnold School study to prove that such diets work. However, conditions in the study were so controlled that few people would be able to repeat them in real life. The study used a small group

Dieting-Induced Weight Gain

Most obese people endure seemingly endless cycles of dieting, losing weight, and regaining it. A 2011 study from Finland came to the conclusion that the obese dieters often gain weight. Experts call this dieting-induced weight gain. This effect was seen when Finnish researchers studied 2,000 sets of overweight identical twins ages 16 to 25. In each case one twin was put on a strict diet while the other twin was not. After a year the dieting twins were two to three times more likely to regain more weight than they lost. This made them heavier than their nondieting twin. And every time test subjects went on a new diet, their weight increased even more. The researchers say, "It is now well established that the more people engage in dieting, the more they gain weight in the long-term."

Quoted in K.H. Pietiläinen, S.E. Saarni, et al., "Does Dieting Make You Fat? A Twin Study," *International Journal of Obesity*, March 2012. www.nature.com.

Animal protein is important because it helps build muscle and maintain bone health.

of people under strict clinical conditions. Complex vegan recipes were cooked by experts. The weight of subjects was checked by doctors. Statistics show that whatever a person's weight, most people have no desire to live on veggies, tofu, and brown rice. According to a 2012 Gallup poll, only 2 percent of Americans are vegans. That number has stayed steady for decades.

Obesity Is "Stamped In"

Diets of any kind rarely work for the severely obese. This is because of their physical makeup. Doctor Richard Atkinson studied the obese for 30 years. He says, "Not all fat people eat too much. . . . [The] body of the obese person is very different from that of a lean person."[23] When the obese diet, their bodies stop using calories for fuel. They become very tired and cannot think clearly. It is hard for them to move around. Whatever calories are consumed are used to boost fat storage. As a result, obese people sometimes gain weight when dieting. Christopher N. Ochner is a weight-management expert. He says, "Once obesity is established ... body weight seems to become biologically 'stamped in' and defended. . . . The depressing fact is that the average adult with . . . obesity has less than a 1% chance of attaining and maintaining a healthy body weight."[24]

Because of genetics, people cannot change how tall they are or the color of their eyes. For the same reason, the obese cannot change their weight simply by dieting.

Concluding Arguments

Many people think that if the obese try hard enough to stick to a strict diet, they will be able to lose weight. Research has shown that the vegan diet can help people lose weight without feeling hungry. But even when the obese lose weight through dieting, they often regain it in a year or two. Experts say this is all too common. The bodies of the obese are programmed to stay at a high weight no matter what they eat. With new diet plans published every day and scientists studying the physical makeup of the obese, the debate over diet and genetics continues.

Examine the Opinions

Examples

Examples are often used to make points or build arguments. They often come from current events, scientific research, and personal stories. In the first essay, the author takes examples from a diet study done by the Arnold School of Public Health. The examples make the point that vegan diets can help the obese lose weight. In the second essay, the author uses examples from scientific research that show how obese people are fighting an uphill battle against their genetic makeup when they attempt to diet.

Convincing writers will include real-world examples to support their point of view. Good examples can change a person's mind and help a debater win an argument. Examples that are not convincing or based on opinion may only offer weak arguments that can easily be refuted.

Wrap It Up!

In this book the authors supply many opinions about obesity. These opinions can be used to write a short essay on the topic. Writing an opinion essay is a good way to look at both sides of an issue. Writers of essays can either express their pro or con opinions or try to find middle ground. The authors used several debate techniques and supplied facts and figures to back their arguments. Cause and effect, appeals to emotion, and the use of examples were techniques used to sway the reader in this book. Any of these could be used in a piece of writing.

There are 6 steps to follow when writing an essay:

Step One: Choose a Topic

When writing your essay, first choose a topic. You can start with one of the three chapter questions from the table of contents in this book.

Step Two: Choose Your Theme

Decide which side of the issue you will take. After choosing your topic, use the materials in this book to write the thesis, or theme, of your essay. You can use the titles of the articles in this book or the sidebar titles as examples of themes. The first paragraph should state your theme. In an essay titled "Snack Foods Are Not to Blame for Obesity," express your opinion. State your ideas that link obesity to sedentary lifestyles and poor overall dietary choices. You could also use a short anecdote, or story, that proves your point and will interest your reader.

Step Three: Research Your Topic

You will need to do some further research to find enough material for your topic. You can find useful books and articles to look up in the bibliography and the notes of this book. Be sure to cite your sources, using the notes at the back of this book as an example.

Step Four: The Body of the Essay

In the next three paragraphs, develop this theme. To do this, come up with three reasons why snack foods are not to blame for obesity. For instance, three reasons could be:

- Eating fattening food is a matter of personal choice.
- People will not become obese from snacks as long as they exercise.
- Snacks should be part of a balanced, healthy diet that includes fruits and vegetables.

These three ideas should each be given their own paragraph. Be sure to give a piece of evidence in each paragraph. This could be a testimonial from a person who cites personal responsibility. Or it could be a story from someone who lost weight by switching to a daily exercise regimen. Each paragraph should end with a transition sentence that sums up the main idea in the paragraph and moves the reader to the next one.

Step Five: Write the Conclusion

The final, or fifth, paragraph should state your conclusion. This should restate your theme and sum up the ideas in your essay. It could also end with an engaging quote or piece of evidence that wraps up your essay.

Step Six: Review Your Work

Finally, be sure to reread your essay. Does it have quotes, facts, and/or anecdotes to support your conclusions? Are your ideas clearly presented? Have another reader take a look at it to see whether someone else can understand your ideas. Make any changes that you think can help make your essay better.

Congratulations on using the ideas in this book to write a personal essay!

Notes

Chapter 1: What Are the Issues with Obesity?

1. Courtney E. Martin, "Separating Fact from Fiction in the Age of Obesity," AlterNet, May 23, 2007. www.alternet.org.
2. Quoted in R. Morgan Griffin, "Obesity Epidemic 'Astronomical,'" WebMD, 2015. www.webmd.com.
3. Quoted in *Wall Street Journal*, "The Experts: What Role Should Government Play in Combatting Obesity?," April 21, 2013. www.wsj.com.
4. American Beverage Association, "Soft Drinks & Diet Soft Drinks," 2012. www.ameribev.org.

Chapter 2: Is Obesity the Fault of the Food Industry?

5. Paul J. Kenny, "Is Obesity an Addiction?," *Scientific American*, August 20, 2013. www.scientificamerican.com.
6. Kenny, "Is Obesity an Addiction?"
7. Quoted in Michael Moss, "The Extraordinary Science of Addictive Junk Food," *New York Times*, February 20, 2013. www.nytimes.com.
8. Quoted in Moss, "The Extraordinary Science of Addictive Junk Food."
9. Quoted in Julia Sommerfeld, "Fat Suits: Who's to Blame for Flab?," NBC News, 2013. www.nbcnews.com.
10. Quoted in Linda Thrasybule, "Junk Food Might Not Be Addictive, After All," Fox News, March 25, 2013. www.foxnews.com.
11. Quoted in Thrasybule, "Junk Food Might Not Be Addictive, After All."

12. Quoted in David Pesci, "Fast Food Not the Major Cause of Rising Childhood Obesity Rates, Study Finds," Gillings School of Global Public Health, December 16, 2013. http://sph.unc.edu.

Chapter 3: Can the Government Prevent Obesity?

13. Quoted in David Lazarus, "A National Soda Tax Is Needed to Reduce Obesity and Save Lives," *Los Angeles Times*, December 8, 2014. www.latimes.com.

14. Quoted in Alice Park, "It's the Ads, Stupid: Why TV Leads to Obesity," *Time*, June 27, 2011. http://healthland.time.com.

15. Quoted in Ted Johnson, "Michelle Obama Calls on Media Companies to Limit Junk Food Ads," *Variety*, September 18, 2013. http://variety.com.

16. Quoted in Beylen Linnekin, "There's Nothing SWEET About the National Soda Tax," *Reason*, August 23, 2014. http://reason.com.

17. Quoted in Ermine Saner, "How Fruit Juice Went from Health Food to Junk Food," *Guardian* (Manchester), January 17, 2014. www.theguardian.com.

18. Quoted in Karen Faster, "Research Finds Soda Tax Does Little to Decrease Obesity," University of Wisconsin–Madison, March 24, 2014. www.news.wisc.edu.

Chapter 4: Is Dieting an Effective Treatment for Obesity?

19. Quoted in Daisy Dumas, "How I Lost 500 Pounds: Morbidly Obese Mother Reveals Her Stunning Transformation," *Daily Mail* (London), February 1, 2012. www.dailymail.co.uk.

20. Gabrielle Turner-McGrievy, "Arnold School Study: Effects of Varying Plant-Based Diets on Weight Loss," Center for Research

in Nutrition and Health Disparities, November 13, 2014.
http://nutritioncenter.sph.sc.edu.

21. Quoted in WebMD, "10 Tips for Losing 100 Pounds or More,"
2015. www.webmd.com.

22. Quoted in Columbia University Medical Center, "Lisa Goetze Gets Going with Gastric Bypass Surgery," 2013.
www.columbiasurgery.org.

23. Quoted in Robin Marantz Henig, "Fat Factors," *New York Times*,
August 13, 2006. www.nytimes.com.

24. Quoted in Melissa Healy, "Diet and Exercise Alone Are No Cure for
Obesity," *Los Angeles Times*, February 13, 2015. www.latimes.com.

Glossary

anticipation: The action of expecting that something is going to happen.

calories: Units of energy contained in food; nutritional requirements are often expressed in calories per day.

hormone: A substance produced in the body that stimulates certain moods, behaviors, or actions.

litigate: To take a claim or dispute into a court of law.

obesity: The condition of being extremely overweight; having too much body fat.

osteoarthritis: A deterioration of hip, knee, ankle, and other joints and surrounding cartilage due to obesity or advanced age.

overweight: The condition of having more body fat than is considered healthy; a person with a body mass index (BMI) between 25 and 30.

regulations: Government rules or laws meant to produce an outcome, such as limiting pollution, that otherwise would not occur.

suppressing: Preventing or slowing an action.

Bibliography

Books

Toney Allman, *Obesity.* Mankato, MN: Cherry Lake, 2014.

Autumn Libal, *Fast Food & the Obesity Epidemic.* Broomall, PA: Mason Crest, 2014.

Websites

Kids' Health (www.cyh.com/HealthTopics/HealthTopicDetailsKids.aspx?p=335&np=152&id=2462). This section of the Kids' Health website explains many aspects of childhood obesity.

Obesity Action Coalition (www.obesityaction.org). This website covers many issues related to obesity.

Index

About the Author

Stuart A. Kallen is the author of more than 300 books for children and young adults. He lives in San Diego, where he hikes, bikes, and plays guitar in his spare time.

16(o)

97 93